BEST OF Sam Phillips

Photography by Eric Gorfain

ISBN 978-1-4234-9942-8

7777 W. BLUEMOUND RD. P.O. BOX 13819 MILWAUKEE, WI 53213

In Australia Contact:
Hal Leonard Australia Pty. Ltd.
4 Lentara Court
Cheltenham, Victoria, 3192 Australia
Email: ausadmin@halleonard.com.au

Visit Hal Leonard Online at
www.halleonard.com

BIOGRAPHY

Anyone who's ever seen Sam Phillips live can't help but be struck by what a world of ideas and emotions she communicates with what seems like so little: a raised eyebrow, a focused glance, a sly smile, an ever-so-subtle turn of her head. Above all, there's her green eyes wide open, as she appears to expand them to their physical limit to take in everyone and everything within their panoramic view.

In many ways, her style is the antithesis of the template for the contemporary hyperkinetic pop star, but it's a perfect manifestation of what Phillips also does so skillfully as a songwriter: capturing, with relentlessly refined clarity, all the wonder and mystery of the life around and within her.

Early on, in a pure-pop gem like "Baby I Can't Please You," she demonstrated her keen grasp of the building blocks of a great pop song, absorbing traditions from both sides of the Atlantic: the expert craftsmanship of Brill Building pros such as Carole King and Ellie Greenwich, as well as the emotional exuberance and musical invention characteristic of the Lennon-McCartney canon.

But launching her career in the 1980s, Phillips also displayed her appreciation for the poetically and spiritually attuned self-reflection that Joni Mitchell, James Taylor, Van Morrison, Laura Nyro and Tom Waits brought to their music.

Indeed, there's long been an artfully couched spiritual dimension to much of her music, whether in the outward expression of an inner thirst for truth in "I Need Love" to the more oblique recognition of the conditions under which new understanding can emerge, tapped so poignantly in "One Day Late."

That perspective carries into and through her explorations of interpersonal relationships. It's all too easy for a writer, who after all is in complete control of the world she conjures in a song, to lob hand grenades of blame at another; far rarer, thus infinitely more valuable, to do as Phillips does in "Strawberry Road" and "If I Could Write," in which she sees clearly within and honestly shares her own insecurities, prejudices, fears, hopes and needs. Life and love aren't simply a series of ups and downs, emotional highs and lows; in Phillips' eyes, they're fundamental facets of the grand mystery we have the opportunity to participate in—if we have the courage to truly embrace it.

Over time she has developed a singular approach to writing that allows her songs to live in a space that's distinctly her own: contemporary, yet timeless; astutely aware of the past, but not beholden to it. "The Fan Dance" adroitly conjures a captivating world of exotic, provocative imagery: "When I do the fan dance/Searchlights answer gunfire/Angels escort falling mercies/Hearts shut off like streetlights."

Like Picasso with his line drawings, Phillips gives the word "economy" a good name, investing the utmost thought, feeling and care into each word, each phrase she chooses—or, perhaps, that choose her.

It's no mystery why T Bone Burnett chose to use "Reflecting Light" as the musical backdrop for the central scene of unguarded romance in the film *Crazy Heart*. It's also not in the least surprising why Alison Krauss and Robert Plant were drawn to the haunting ambience of "Sister Rosetta Goes Before Us," with its compelling "yin-yang" toggling between major and minor melodic motifs, for their transcendent *Raising Sand* collaboration.

Phillips' evolution as an artist is apparent in the nearly two-decade span of the songs in this collection. She has taken to heart the Zen-like mindset of the sculptor; viewing her life experience as a raw block of stone or wood, not with the attitude of what she and her will can impose on it, but to discern what natural form lurks within it. Once perceived, she sets about chipping away everything that doesn't belong, leaving behind only what's absolutely essential.

Phillips' songs emerge as exquisitely formed pieces that share a defining quality of the most enduring artworks: the feeling that they somehow needed to exist.

"Going down this road," she writes in "Love is Everywhere I Go," "I finally know there is no end to the good."

As much as such songs needed Sam Phillips to bring them into the world, the truth is, the world needs Sam Phillips just as much to keep bringing them.

Randy Lewis
Los Angeles Times

I THINK ABOUT YOU EVERY DAY.

Health and happiness are
coming your way.
3 10 20 34 41, 21

I love writing songs. I started writing songs to change the world, but writing songs changed me.

I am happy these songs have found their way to you and hope you enjoy them — all the best from Sam

Sam Phillips

CONTENTS

ALL NIGHT

Words and Music by
SAM PHILLIPS

BABY I CAN'T PLEASE YOU

Words and Music by
SAM PHILLIPS

DON'T DO ANYTHING

Words and Music by
SAM PHILLIPS

EDGE OF THE WORLD

Words and Music by
SAM PHILLIPS

To Coda

FAN DANCE

Words and Music by
SAM PHILLIPS

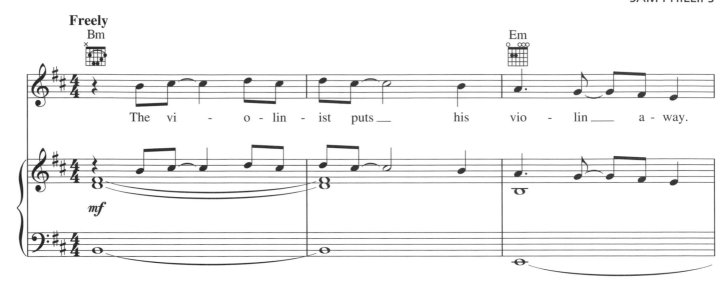

The vi-o-lin-ist puts ___ his vio-lin ___ a-way.

For-bid-den ci-ty bro-ken in-to to-night.

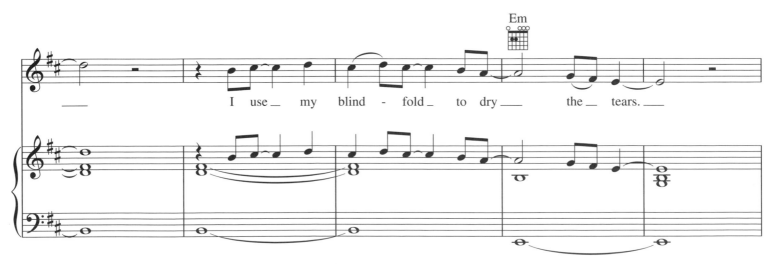

I use ___ my blind-fold to dry ___ the ___ tears. ___

HOW TO DREAM

Words and Music by
SAM PHILLIPS

IF I COULD WRITE

Words and Music by
SAM PHILLIPS

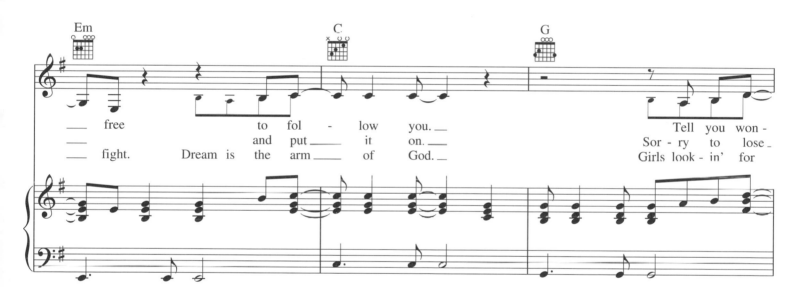

I NEED LOVE

Words and Music by
SAM PHILLIPS

LOVE IS EVERYWHERE I GO

Words and Music by
SAM PHILLIPS

ONE DAY LATE

Words and Music by
SAM PHILLIPS

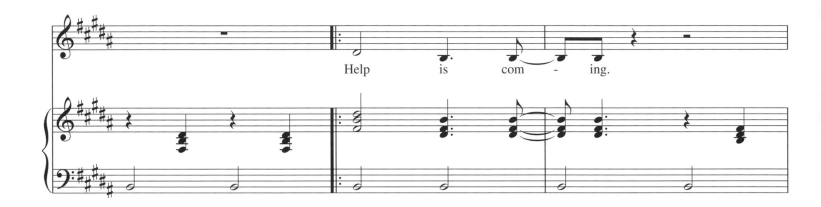

Help is com - ing.

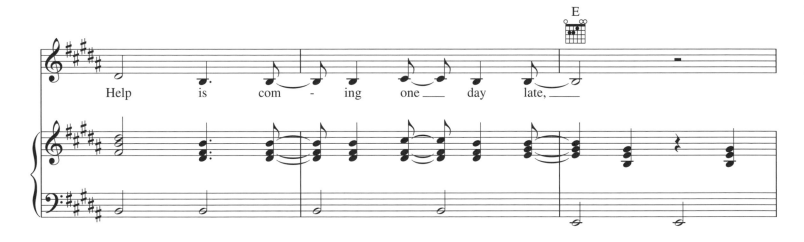

Help is com - ing one ____ day late, ____

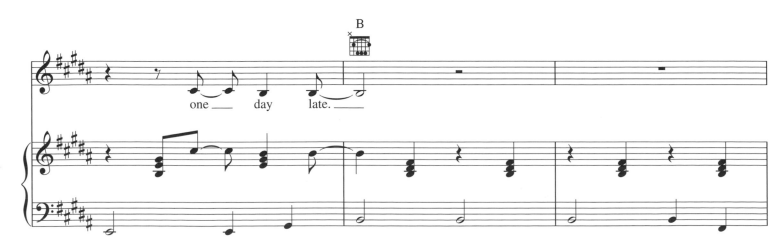

one ____ day late. ____

REFLECTING LIGHT

Words and Music by
SAM PHILLIPS

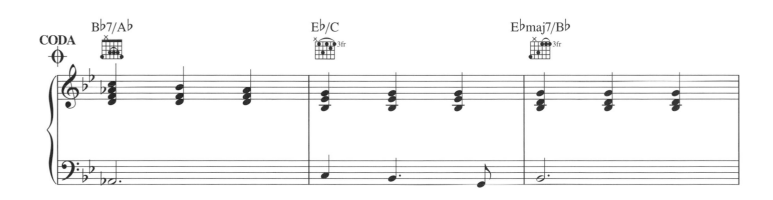

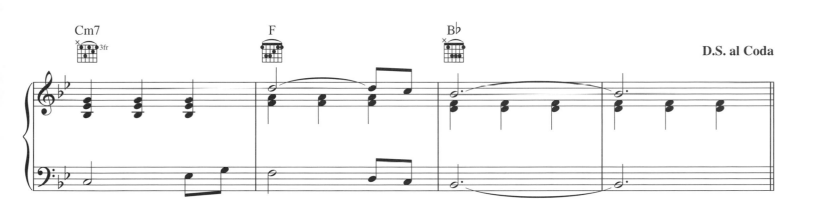

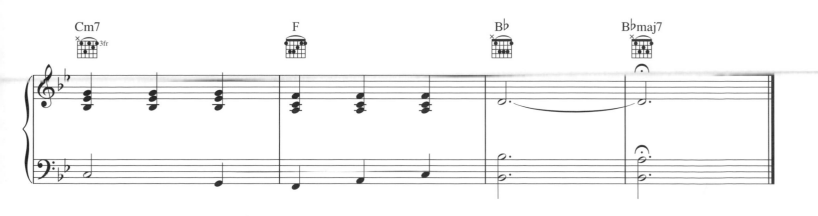

SAY WHAT YOU MEAN

Words and Music by SAM PHILLIPS
and T-BONE BURNETT

I'll be des-'prate, __ I'll be lone-ly, ___ but I

Instrumental

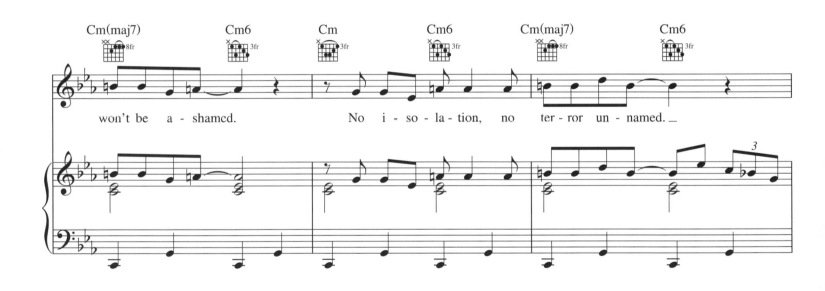

won't be a-shamed. No i-so-la-tion, no ter-ror un-named. __

You an-i-mat-ed the dead to your dream. __ Say what you mean. __

SIGNAL

Words and Music by
SAM PHILLIPS

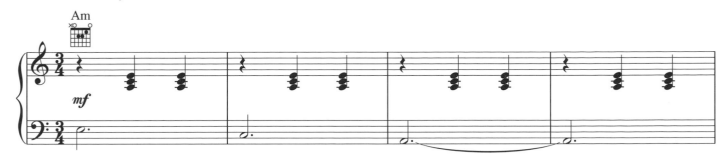

The streets _____ are your bro-ken
Find - ing

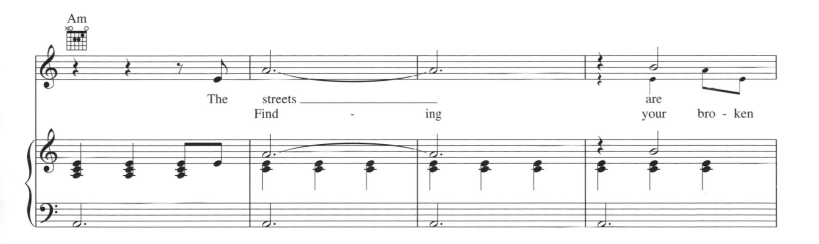

so dark at night. _____
heart and fall - ing in.

through the shoul-ders where the wings might have

been.

SISTER ROSETTA GOES BEFORE US

Words and Music by
SAM PHILLIPS

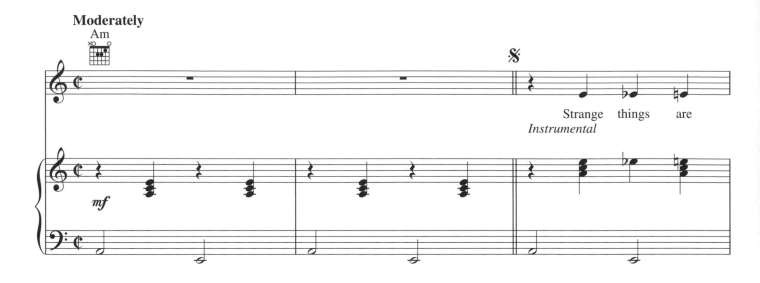

Strange things are Instrumental

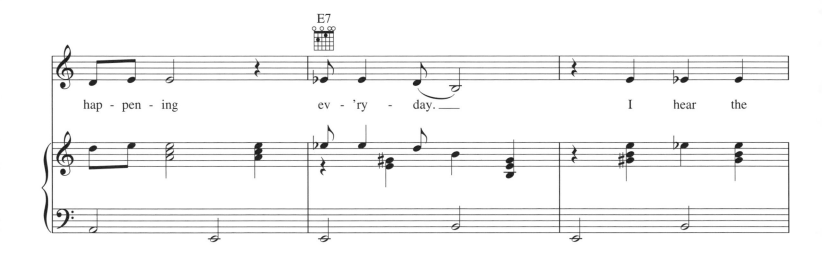

hap - pen - ing ev - 'ry - day. ___ I hear the

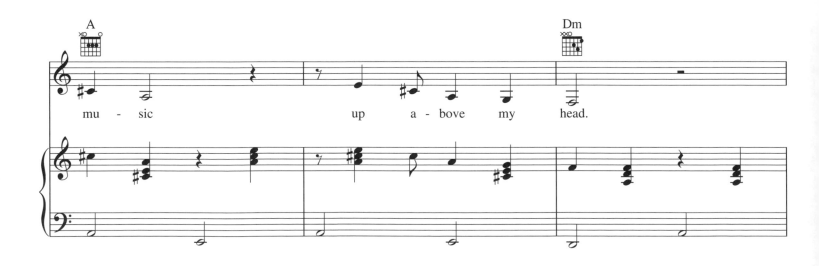

mu - sic up a - bove my head.

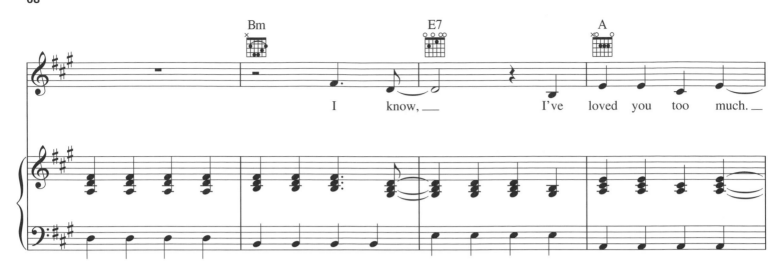

I know, ___ I've loved you too much. ___

___ I'll ___ go on ___ a - lone ___ to get through.

D.S. al Coda

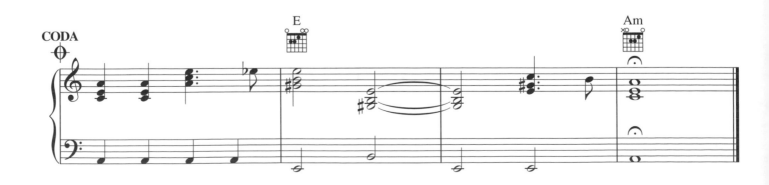

CODA

STRAWBERRY ROAD

Words and Music by
SAM PHILLIPS

SO GLAD YOU'RE HERE

Words and Music by
SAM PHILLIPS

WHERE THE COLORS DON'T GO

Words and Music by
SAM PHILLIPS